Gaming Gray Zone Tactics

Design Considerations for a Structured Strategic Game

BECCA WASSER, JENNY OBERHOLTZER,
STACIE L. PETTYJOHN, WILLIAM MACKENZIE

Prepared for the United States Army
Approved for public release; distribution unlimited

For more information on this publication, visit www.rand.org/t/RR2915

Library of Congress Cataloging-in-Publication Data is available for this publication.
ISBN: 978-1-9774-0401-5

Published by the RAND Corporation, Santa Monica, Calif.
© Copyright 2019 RAND Corporation
RAND® is a registered trademark.

www.rand.org

Preface

This report documents research and analysis conducted as part of a project entitled *Gray Zone War Games*, sponsored by the Office of the Deputy Chief of Staff, G-3/5/7, U.S. Army. The purpose of the project was to develop an interrelated series of expert input, tabletop, and computer-assisted war games to simulate "gray zone" tactics or measures short of war, to develop activities to support analysis of strategic and operational threats and opportunities, to inform indications and warning processes, and to support U.S., UK, and other allied strategies and force development plans.

This research was conducted within the RAND Arroyo Center's Strategy, Doctrine, and Resources Program. RAND Arroyo Center, part of the RAND Corporation, is a federally funded research and development center sponsored by the United States Army. RAND's publications do not necessarily reflect the opinions of its research clients and sponsors.

RAND operates under a "Federal-Wide Assurance" (FWA00003425) and complies with the *Code of Federal Regulations for the Protection of Human Subjects Under United States Law* (45 CFR 46), also known as "the Common Rule," as well as with the implementation guidance set forth in Department of Defense (DoD) Instruction 3216.02. As applicable, this compliance includes reviews and approvals by RAND's Institutional Review Board (the Human Subjects Protection Committee) and by the U.S. Army. The views of sources utilized in this study are solely their own and do not represent the official policy or position of DoD or the U.S. Government.

Contents

Figures and Table

Figures

Table

Summary

The gray zone is a murky concept, touted as a new paradigm of geo-strategic competition and used to describe the variety of challenges that the United States presently faces in light of broader shifts in the international order. It is characterized by adversaries challenging the United States politically, economically, informationally, and militarily while remaining under the threshold of war. As the world has returned to an era of great-power competition, the rate of gray zone conflicts has risen as such adversaries as Russia have increasingly sought to challenge the United States indirectly through gray zone tactics.

Russia's use of gray zone tactics in Europe preys on existing vulnerabilities to polarize populations, states, and institutions, while intentionally obfuscating the source and intent of such actions. Russian gray zone aggression has risen in recent years, spurred by viable successes in the Donbass and Crimea regions of Ukraine in 2014. Although Russia's use of conventional and unconventional tools seemingly presents a new challenge to the United States, measures short of war are not new.

To better understand the nature of a gray zone competition with Russia, we developed a strategic-level structured card game examining a gray zone competition between Russia and the West in the Balkans. In these games, the Russian player seeks to expand its influence and undermine North Atlantic Treaty Organization unity while competing against a European team and a U.S. team seeking to defend their allies from Russia's gray zone activities without provoking an outright war. This report details the development of this game and our research approach. In it, we discuss key design decisions, elements of the game, and how the game is played. We conclude with a discussion of the limitations of the game, and recommendations for future applications of the game design.

Key findings from playing this war game with subject-matter experts can be found in a companion report, *Competing in the Gray Zone: Russian Tactics and Western Responses.*

Acknowledgments

The authors thank MG William Hix and MG Christopher McPadden for the opportunity to examine an important question, and MAJ Robert Kurtts for his guidance of the project. We are grateful to Michael Markowitz from the Center for Naval Analyses and Karl Mueller from the RAND Corporation for their helpful comments on an earlier draft of this report. At RAND, we would like to extend thanks to our colleagues Stephanie Pezard, Ben Connable, David Frelinger, Leah Hershey, and David Shlapak for their support in the development of these games; Rachel Ostrow for her masterful editing; and Sally Sleeper and Jennifer Kavanagh for their guidance of the project. We also thank the players in the multiple games we play-tested and conducted at RAND for their participation and valuable insights.

Abbreviations

BPC	building partner capacity
CRT	combat results table
DIME	diplomatic, information, military, and economic
EU	European Union
MAP	membership action plan
NATO	North Atlantic Treaty Organization
SME	subject-matter expert
UN	United Nations

CHAPTER ONE

Introduction

Gray zone has become a catchall phrase to describe the current operating environment and the variety of challenges that the United States faces in light of broader shifts in the global order. A nebulous concept at best, the gray zone is characterized by adversaries challenging the United States politically, economically, informationally, and militarily while remaining under the threshold of war.[1] The gray zone concept has gained traction within the U.S. government and wider policy and academic communities as a new paradigm of geostrategic competition. However, there is a complex debate among analysts over the validity of the gray zone concept, including its very existence, composition, and strategic merit.[2] The murky nature of the gray zone has reinforced broad definitions and enabled the concept to become a repository for a diverse array of challenges, ranging from territorial expansion to electoral interference to economic coercion.

---

[1] The National Defense Strategy refers to efforts "short of armed conflict" while National Security Strategy refers to "below the threshold of open conflict" (Donald J. Trump, *National Security Strategy of the United States of America*, Washington, D.C.: The White House, December 2017; U.S. Department of Defense, *Summary of the 2018 National Defense Strategy of the United States of America: Sharpening the American Military's Competitive Edge*, Washington, D.C., January 2018).

[2] See, for example, the debate between Adam Elkus and Michael J. Mazarr at War on the Rocks: Adam Elkus, "50 Shades of Gray: Why the Gray Wars Concept Lacks Strategic Sense," *War on the Rocks*, December 15, 2015a; Adam Elkus, "Abandon All Hope, Ye Who Enter Here: You Cannot Save the Gray Zone Concept," *War on the Rocks*, December 30, 2015b; and Michael J. Mazarr, "Struggle in the Gray Zone and World Order," *War on the Rocks*, December 22, 2015.

We define gray zone tactics as *ambiguous* political, economic, informational, or military actions that primarily target domestic or international public opinion and are employed to advance a nation's interests while still aiming to avoid retaliation, escalation, or third-party intervention. Note that we focus on gray zone *tactics* as opposed to the gray zone as a distinct type or sphere of conflict. We assert that it is both intellectually more coherent and, for the policymaker, more operationally useful to conceptualize the gray zone as a type of tactic rather than a unique form of conflict or operating environment.

Russia is cited as one of the greatest threats to the U.S.-dominated global order and is a top competitor using gray zone tactics today.[3] Examples of Russian gray zone actions include interference in the 2016 U.S. presidential election; Moscow's annexation of the Crimean peninsula; the use of "little green men"[4] in Ukraine in 2014; and the 2007 cyberattacks on Estonian financial, media, and government institutions. Additionally, Russia undertakes lower-profile subversive acts—such as financial support to separatist movements, local disinformation campaigns, and co-opting of critical economic sectors.[5] In all these cases, Russian actions exploit existing vulnerabilities in an effort to keep its neighbors weak and compliant, undercut U.S. interests, and divide European allies while maintaining plausible deniability.

The rate and frequency with which Russia has employed gray zone tactics has risen in recent years. Moscow has taken advantage of its ties to post-Soviet states, which are plagued by weak governance and rule of law, to exploit vulnerabilities and further erode government institutions. In an effort to stop Montenegro's accession into the North Atlantic Treaty Organization (NATO), in 2016, Russia employed an array of gray zone tactics in a plot to overthrow the Montenegrin gov-

---

[3]   President Donald J. Trump, 2017; U.S. Department of Defense, 2018.

[4]   *Little green men* is the term used for armed men wearing uniforms without insignia, who had purported ties to Russian armed forces, during the Ukraine crisis and annexation of Crimea.

[5]   A larger list of examples is included in Stacie L. Pettyjohn and Becca Wasser, *Competing in the Gray Zone: Russian Tactics and Western Responses,* Santa Monica, Calif.: RAND Corporation, RR-2791-A, 2019.

ernment.[6] Even long-standing NATO members, largely composed of more-resilient Western European states, have not been immune to Russian gray zone activities.[7] Although there are commonalities across these cases, Russia's use of gray zone tactics has varied and depended on the target and the tools available to Moscow. The variation in Russia's gray zone tool kit has only added to the ambiguous nature of such tactics, and has made it difficult for the United States and its European allies to counter such acts.

The lack of a consensus definition for the gray zone has complicated existing research efforts to understand its character and how adversaries use gray zone tactics. The muddled concept has, in turn, made it difficult to identify how to combat gray zone aggression. The broad variety of activities that fall under the gray zone umbrella and the dynamic nature of the competition between the West and Russia require an effort to parse the concept in a systematic manner. We developed a structured, strategic-level gray zone game to help to overcome these challenges, which we played several times with RAND Corporation experts on European, Russian, and U.S. defense and intelligence policy. This game modeled gray zone tactics and how they could be employed in Europe, specifically in a Balkans scenario. The game acted as a vehicle to understand gray zone competition in Europe, including the potential roles that the United States, NATO, and the European Union (EU) might play in such a competition.[8]

This report describes the Balkans gray zone game in greater detail. It is divided into three parts. First, we describe our research approach and the rationale for a structured game.[9] Second, we detail

---

[6] John McCain, "Russia Threat Is Dead Serious. Montenegro Coup and Murder Plot Proves It," *USA Today*, June 29, 2017.

[7] Examples include Russian interference in the 2017 French presidential election and the 2016 Brexit vote in the United Kingdom. Matt Burgess, "Here's the First Evidence Russia Used Twitter to Influence Brexit," *Wired*, November 10, 2017; Andy Greenberg, "The NSA Confirms It: Russia Hacked French Election 'Infrastructure,'" *Wired*, May 9, 2017.

[8] Key insights and findings from these games are in Pettyjohn and Wasser, 2019.

[9] There are three types of serious strategy games discussed in this report: free-form games, matrix games, and structured games. Free-form games (also known as seminar-style games) have few rules or physical elements, and game outcomes are determined by expert adjudica-

the elements of the final game and discuss our approach to adjudication. Finally, the report concludes with a discussion of the limitations of the game and potential future applications of the approach.

---

tors in an ad-hoc way. Matrix games are a specific type of argumentation-based game where the teams present reasons why they could—or their adversary could not—do something, and then an adjudicator or umpire makes a final determination based on the net quality of the argumentation for and against an action. Structured games typically represent the phenomena with physical elements (e.g., cards and blocks) and have rules that determine game outcomes.

CHAPTER TWO

Building a Structured Gray Zone Game

This chapter describes the purpose and process of designing a structured gray zone game. It explains why a structured game was chosen as the best approach to explore Russian gray zone tactics in Europe and the research process that developed the model that underpins the game engine.

Game Purpose

Fundamentally, this game is a tool to explore Russia's use of gray zone tactics and Western responses in the Balkans.[1] Because of the lack of clarity surrounding the gray zone concept and the varied types of actions lumped under this rubric, it is a significant challenge for the United States, NATO, and allied nations to formulate appropriate individual—let alone collective—responses to address Russia's ambiguous hostile actions. The intent of the game is to gain a better understanding of the tactics and tools used by adversaries and the tactics and tools available to the United States and its allies, how such tactics and tools can be employed, the tradeoffs associated with different courses of action, and the strengths and weaknesses of different target nations. This game allows players to test out different combinations of activities to gain insights into where and why they might fail or succeed. In sum,

---

[1] Although this particular game is focused on a gray zone competition in Europe, we discuss additional geographic and functional applications of this game platform later in the report.

our gray zone games were intended to serve as vehicles for the players to develop coherent strategies, explore the pros and cons of different decisions, and have a robust discussion that helped them to identify which strategies appear to be effective in different situations and which strategies appear the most robust against a variety of possible futures. This, in turn, will assist the U.S. Army, NATO, the EU, and European governments to identify where they need to focus their efforts and the role different nations and organizations might play in such a competition.

Research Approach

We began our development of the game with an extensive literature review.[2] First, we reviewed books, articles, and white papers written about the gray zone and such related concepts as hybrid war, drawing on academic, policy, and government sources.[3] Because there is not a consensus definition of the gray zone, we systematically tracked and categorized the actions considered to fall into this area; singled out the key characteristics that drove this characterization; and through a comparison of these actions and their characteristics, developed a clear definition of gray zone tactics. This exercise provided us with a strong understanding of what academia, the policy community, and government believe the gray zone to be, and better enabled us to represent these ideas in the game.

Second, we reviewed literature specific to Russian gray zone threats in Europe. This included examining the strengths and weaknesses of different European states and the different forms of influence and gray zone actions that the Kremlin has employed against them in the past. As a part of this exploration, we studied empirical accounts of

---

[2] A substantive discussion and citations are in Pettyjohn and Wasser, 2019.

[3] Although *hybrid warfare* and *gray zone* are not synonymous, they are often conflated or at least described as related concepts. Therefore, researching Russia's approach to hybrid warfare provided us with a better baseline to understand how a gray zone competition might play out in Europe, and the types of gray zone tactics Russia might employ.

the efficacy of these different tactics and identified patterns in factors driving the common outcomes across the cases.

Third, we explored the steps that the United States and European nations have taken to combat gray zone tactics. This provided us with a baseline understanding of what different states and European international organizations are doing to confront these threats and other countermeasures that are being considered.

Designing a Gray Zone Game: Iterative Game Design

The primary challenge to designing a gray zone game is the fact that the gray zone encompasses a large array of different types of political, social, economic, and military actions that are intended to have strategic effects. The absence of clearly defined parameters for what the gray zone is means that a disparate suite of diplomatic, information, military, and economic (DIME) activities must be included in game play. Although it is widely accepted that rules can be created to accurately adjudicate combat outcomes, there is skepticism that the same can be done for social, political, and economic outcomes. According to this view, political and economic factors are far too complex to accurately be modeled in a quantitative fashion.[4]

This is why the default option for most political-military games is to adopt a "free-form" structure, in which formal rule sets are minimized and complexity is incorporated through the mental models of the "expert" players and the "expert" adjudicators. Free-form games provide a scenario that describes the setting or state of the game world and background reference materials to help the players to make decisions. Game play centers around teams role-playing different nations and participating in seminar-style discussions, where they consider the situation, deliberate, and ultimately decide what they will do in response to the situation that they face. An expert control team then

---

[4] Herbert Goldhamer and Hans Speier, "Some Observations on Political Gaming," *World Politics*, Vol. 12, No. 1, October 1959.

takes the inputs from all teams (usually two) and determines whether and how their moves interact and what effect their actions will have.[5]

Given the complexity of the topic that we were exploring, we planned on running a series of war games with each game building on what was learned in the earlier exercises and coupling these lessons learned with additional research to gradually create a structured game with a fully specified set of rules for adjudicating outcomes and guiding player actions. We aspired to create a structured game because of the limitations of free-form games that we had experienced previously and which ended up materializing in the early gray zone games: This included ad hoc and inconsistent adjudication, unfocused player deliberations, and unconstrained decisionmaking.

Structured games require rigid rules or an undergirding model, which, when a problem is poorly understood, is difficult—if not impossible—to create. A gray zone competition—given the confusion and debate over what the gray zone is and is not—would therefore seem to be nearly impossible to model in a structured game. However, although the gray zone might be touted as a new paradigm of conflict, most of the tactics employed in this type of competition are not new.[6] George Kennan discussed the concept of measures short of war in 1946; the difference today is simply in the instrumentalities employed, because the tools used have adapted with the times.[7] Because these individual actions have been studied, this knowledge can be folded into a simple model and incorporated into a game to adjudicate social,

---

[5] For more on free-form political-military games, see Lincoln P. Bloomfield, *Political Gaming*, Carlisle, Pa.: US Army War College, November 20, 1959; William M. Jones, *On Free-Form Gaming*, Santa Monica, Calif.: RAND Corporation, N-2322-RC, 1985; and Robert Levine, Thomas Schelling, and William M. Jones, *Crisis Games 27 Years Later: Plus C'est Deja Vu*, Santa Monica, Calif.: RAND Corporation, P-7719, 1991.

[6] See Hal Brands, "Paradoxes of the Gray Zone," Foreign Policy Research Institute, February 5, 2016.

[7] Giles D. Harlow and George C. Maerz, eds., *Measures Short of War: The George F. Kennan Lectures at the National War College, 1946-1947*, Washington, D.C.: National Defense University Press, 1991.

political, and economic outcomes.[8] Creating the structured game was an iterative process that involved extensive research on the concept of the gray zone, Russia's unconventional tactics, counteractions to Russian measures, and their effectiveness (see Figure 2.1).

Figure 2.1
Gray Zone Game Design Process

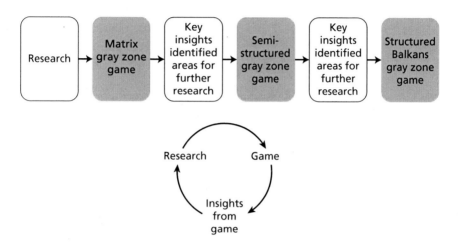

All of our gray zone games included a Russian (Red) team tasked with expanding its influence and undermining NATO unity competing against a European (Green) team and a U.S. (Blue) team aiming to defend their allies from Russia's gray zone activities without provoking an outright war. The players in our games were a diverse group of RAND experts on Russian, European, and U.S. defense and intel-

---

[8] In addition to Kennan, see Thomas Wright, *All Measures Short of War: The Contest for the Twenty-First Century and the Future of American Power*, New Haven, Conn.: Yale University Press, 2017; and Ben Connable, Jason H. Campbell, and Dan Madden, *Stretching and Exploiting Thresholds for High-Order War: How Russia, China, and Iran Are Eroding American Influence Using Time-Tested Measures Short of War*, Santa Monica, Calif.: RAND Corporation, RR-1003-A, 2016.

ligence policy. We purposefully selected players who had the requisite knowledge to role-play U.S., European, or Russian policymakers either trying to defeat or use gray zone tactics to further their interests. Their expertise allowed them to more realistically represent the countries and actors involved in game play. Furthermore, many of these experts are familiar with gaming, which strengthened their ability to play their respective roles effectively.

The first gray zone games were matrix games, which were largely free-form exercises in which the teams made arguments for and against an outcome; these arguments were judged by umpires who probabilistically determined the effects of these actions based on the quality of the arguments.[9] For example, for Russia to interfere in the French presidential election by hacking voting machines, the Red team would argue why this act would be effective. The Blue and Green team, in response, would argue against the effectiveness of this action, potentially citing defensive updates to electoral infrastructure and the widespread use of paper ballots in France. Ultimately, the control team would determine how effective the arguments and counterarguments were by determining a probability of success and then rolling a die to determine the outcome of the action.

We initially opted for this approach as a part of our building-block method for creating the structured game and exploring Russian gray zone tactics. Because the games did not impose many rules on game play, the teams had the latitude to develop innovative and unpredictable strategies.[10] As game designers, we used a more open-ended approach to the early games to ensure that we did not narrow our focus too quickly and leave out important aspects of this issue. We used the games to help to build a wide-ranging list of Russian, U.S., and European actions so that they could be incorporated into the structured game. Because matrix games force the players to pres-

---

[9]   For more information on matrix games, see John Curry and Tim Price, *Matrix Games for Modern Wargaming: Developments in Professional and Educational Wargames, Innovations in Wargaming*, Vol. 2, Barking, UK: Lulu Press, Inc., August 2014.

[10]   Bloomfield, 1959, pp. 6, 8, 17; Thomas Schelling, "An Uninhibited Sales Pitch for Crisis Games," in Levine, Schelling, and Jones, 1991, pp. 22–23.

ent arguments as to why their actions would or would not succeed, these games also helped us to begin to identify the causal logic—the underlying models—that would determine the outcomes of different tactics.[11] Finally, the matrix games aided the process of focusing and scoping our study. For instance, insights from these early games led us to limit the geography of the game so that we concentrated on the Balkans, a region that seemed to be an increasingly important target for Russian gray zone aggression.

Yet the matrix games also had several weaknesses that a structured game could address. At times, the players floundered because of the open-ended nature of their task and often were overwhelmed by the vast array of targets, tactics, and strategies they could adopt. In the end, this made it difficult for the players to determine their priorities and hindered the development of coherent strategies. Additionally, the matrix games introduced inconsistencies in terms of how actions were adjudicated across games and sometimes even within a game, making direct comparisons difficult. The players and umpires also struggled to keep track of the different actions that were taken across time in several locations in a systematic way.

In an effort to address some of these shortcomings, we next developed a semistructured game that provided the players with a menu of options and pieces to assist them in their decisionmaking process and a game board to track actions. We also employed a partially specified set of rules for adjudicating outcomes, which were essentially rules of thumb to provide an initial probability that an action would succeed or fail. Players could still increase or decrease this probability using the arguments that they presented to the umpires. Although these actions helped to improve the games and our understanding of Russian gray zone tactics, the semistructured games did not resolve the problems of tracking game play and still allowed too much variability in terms of actions and outcomes. Consequently, we moved on to creating a structured gray zone board game focused on the Balkans.

---

[11] The causal logic presented in the game was then cross-checked through an examination of the literature on the subject.

Structured board games purposefully limit player choices to focus their deliberations on key issues while promoting player engagement with the use of tactile game components.[12] Because ours used simple physical pieces, such as cards, these components could be created quickly and could easily be expanded or improved. Structured games require a model that is realistic enough yet playable enough to determine game outcomes. We created simple rule sets that distilled the existing empirical literature on individual gray zone tactics and countermeasures into a set of probability curves that were represented as a combat results table (CRT). These rules captured the central causal relationships of different phenomena, but were simple enough that they allowed for relatively quick adjudication so that the game could be played in the course of a day. Our adjudication model was simple and transparent, because simplicity was appropriate given the level of knowledge about the phenomena in question and because a simple model could be grasped by the players.[13] Players could understand what contextual factors made actions more or less likely to succeed and also observed when a lucky roll of a die drove specific results.

Transparency also meant that players provided an additional check on our models, which were intended to be decision-support models that helped the players to think about what strategies other teams might employ, the tradeoffs associated with different courses of action, and which actions are more or less plausible under different conditions. Our rules were accessible to the players, as they were printed on cards that were an integral component of the game. Because the players could understand what drove game outcomes, the white cell (or game controllers) elicited the players' expertise and feedback to iteratively improve the rules. Thus, for example, players could argue that we weighted an action—e.g., an attempted covert assassination—with too high a probability of success, using their own expertise. We

---

[12] Structured games include and resemble off-the-shelf commercial games and have physical components (e.g., map, game pieces, cards).

[13] Paul K. Davis and Don Blumenthal, *The Base of Sand Problem: A White Paper on the State of Military Combat Modeling*, Santa Monica, Calif.: RAND Corporation, N-3148-OSD/DARPA, 1991.

would discuss why they believed this to be the case, and if convinced that the rules did not accurately reflect the probability of success, we would modify them. We do not claim that the rules or the underlying relationships are *correct*; rather, they are consistent with the literature and the participating experts' understanding of these phenomena and offer a standard baseline for determining game outcomes. The adjudication was replicable, but the games themselves still are not experiments or quasiexperiments because human players inevitably introduce variability in terms of the strategies that they adopt, the specific actions that they take, and how they frame them.[14]

Within a structured game such as this, there is also a risk that the players mistakenly believe that the stochastic model that determines game outcomes is predictive of what will occur in the real world when, in fact, there is considerable uncertainty about the probabilities. Moreover, because the adjudication often depended on multiple factors, errors could be compounded. To ensure that players did not misinterpret game outcomes, we highlighted the limitations of the game at the outset and conclusion and what the players should and should not take away from the exercise. Additionally, the analysis found in our companion report was not founded solely on game results, but incorporated those results into a larger body of research on Russian gray zone tactics.[15] The next chapter details the different components of the structured Balkans gray zone game.

---

[14] Games are intrinsically nonreplicable because you cannot hold the players constant. Even participants who have played the game before will have learned from that prior experience and therefore aren't the "same" players.

[15] Pettyjohn and Wasser, 2019.

CHAPTER THREE

Balkans Gray Zone Game

This chapter reviews the development and design of a structured gray zone game focusing on the Balkans. It covers key design choices and simplifications and the theoretical approach underpinning the game model before detailing the various elements of the game and game play. This chapter provides a more nuanced understanding of the strengths and limitations of the game.

Structured Balkans Gray Zone Game

The iterative design process for the structured Balkans gray zone game described in Chapter Two helped us better understand gray zone tactics, more adequately refine and scope our research, and highlight important issues for further research. The two earlier games also helped us decide on key mechanics and structure to incorporate into the final game design to improve playability.

Although the two early games had some serious limitations, when paired with additional research, they were useful in generating insights about the nature of gray zone tactics, how these tactics are employed in Europe, and their efficacy against different countries or regions of Europe.[1] We used what we learned about gray zone tactics from these games and existing empirical literature to build a model which represented these tactics and captured the causal relationships of differ-

---

[1] Key insights and findings from playing this game are in Pettyjohn and Wasser, 2019.

ent phenomena. This model underpinned the structured game and enabled us to track complicated and varied actions and interactions between moves, and to systematically and transparently determine outcomes across games, thus producing additional insights relevant to our study questions. This model was built into a strategic-level structured card game examining a gray zone competition between Russia and the West in the Balkans.

Game Design Choices

In the development of the structured game, we made several critical game design choices. The first key decision was to limit the geography of the game. The previous two games allowed free play across all of Europe. Although this produced valuable insights about different types of gray zone tactics and the level and kinds of vulnerabilities in different nations, the wide geography made it difficult for players—particularly those playing Blue and Green—to focus their actions, because they had too many decisions to make in a game that only lasted a day or two. It also complicated efforts to constrain player actions by limiting available resources to make the game a more accurate representation of the real world, where countries and institutions cannot do everything and anything all at once. The broad geography also made it difficult to track the effects of actions, which at times were cumulative, and complicated adjudication, leading certain actions to have outsized impacts on the game. Therefore, we concluded that if we wanted to learn more, we needed to limit the scope of the game.

As a result, we decided to refine the game to focus only on the Balkans.[2] Recent attention has focused on Russian efforts to undermine democracies and the countries in its immediate periphery. The Balkans are less often studied as a battleground for malign Russian activity. There are, however, ample examples of Russian gray zone meddling in

---

[2] In the game, the Balkans are defined as Albania, Bosnia, Bulgaria, Croatia, Kosovo, Macedonia, Montenegro, Romania, Serbia, and Slovenia.

these countries.[3] NATO and the EU are seeking to incorporate new members from the Balkans, making it a ripe area to explore how gray zone tactics might play out.[4] Moreover, in our early games, Blue and Green players identified the Balkans as a region vulnerable to Russian gray zone tactics because of poor governance, rampant corruption, and sectarian divisions, although the Red players saw this area as one of increasing concern because more Balkan nations were considering joining Western institutions, which Moscow viewed as threatening.

Furthermore, from the standpoint of our study, the Balkans provide a more interesting test environment than Western Europe because Russia has demonstrated that it is able and willing to use a wide variety of gray zone tactics in the Balkans. As reflected in the early games, different regions possess unique vulnerabilities to gray zone tactics, and Russia emphasizes different types of tactics in each region accordingly. In Western Europe, Russia mainly tends to use "everyday" nonviolent gray zone actions aiming to court allies and shape public opinion, and occasionally undertakes targeted, nonviolent campaigns to affect specific events, especially elections. In the Balkans, Russian gray zone tactics range from these "everyday" actions to higher-order violent acts, and therefore provide us with a more complete environment to examine the use and efficacy of gray zone tactics and the available countermeasures.[5]

The second design choice was to make the game into a three-sided game, with players representing Russia, the United States, and Europe, to promote playability. The Green player represents all of Europe, including both NATO and the EU. It should be noted that the U.S. and Russian teams were tasked with playing at the national level, rather than trying to represent the differences between a variety of stakeholders within each nation. However, we asked the subject-matter experts (SMEs) playing Green to honestly represent the differ-

---

[3] Pettyjohn and Wasser, 2019.

[4] For more recent examples of Russian gray zone activity in the Balkans, see Steven Erlanger, "In a New Cold War with Russia, Balkans Become a Testing Ground," *New York Times*, April 10, 2018.

[5] Pettyjohn and Wasser, 2019.

ent perspectives and capabilities of European countries by undertaking only actions that were plausible given their understanding of European states' politics, policies, and viewpoints. These SMEs therefore called out when certain NATO or EU member states would be reticent to agree to a specific action or noted when an act would need to be carried out by a "coalition of the willing" in light of differences among alliance member states. This allowed us to incorporate intra-European differences, which are an important constraint on efforts to counter Russian gray zone tactics, while keeping the game from becoming overly complicated and unplayable. Additionally, because our study was sponsored by the U.S. Army and we were interested in understanding what role it should play in countering Russian gray zone tactics, intra-European differences were an important factor but not the focus.[6]

The decision to develop a three-sided game introduced additional complexity. We considered modeling Green in the game so that it was not an independent player but rather integrated into the game mechanics in a predetermined fashion. However, we ultimately decided against this approach because it would have complicated the game mechanics considerably, and would have reduced our ability to differentiate between what the United States and European nations and institutions could and should do to counter Russian gray zone actions. Additionally, a two-player game would not have been able to explore the issues of transatlantic and European unity, which are a target of Russian gray zone tactics.

The third design choice focused on the representation of time. As many gray zone tactics are not intended to have immediate effects, but rather to be investments that pay off over time, we needed simultaneously to represent both incremental, long-term strategies and more targeted urgent efforts. Therefore, we decided to build a timeline as the main game board, with a long-term and a short-term track. In the former, players develop a long-term strategy and implement actions that will occur over the course of a year; the latter allows for more immediate actions and counters that players make in 3-month incre-

---

[6] However, future iterations of this game could give greater attention to intra-European differences because this would produce interesting insights about NATO unity.

ments. This approach eased the task of tracking gradualist strategies and the interplay between combinations of tactics.

The fourth critical design choice we made was the inclusion of both a wide variety of gray zone tactics and other measures short of war, including some that did not fit our definition of gray zone tactics.[7] For gray zone tactics, these ranged from disinformation campaigns to financially backing foreign political parties to covert attempts to overthrow a government. Non–gray zone tactics included economic sanctions and building partner law enforcement capacity. We did not limit the teams to only gray zone tactics or inform them about our definition—we wanted to explore whether gray zone tactics alone or in combination with other types of actions had the greatest effect. At the same time, because our gray zone game was designed to explore competition below the threshold of major war, we did not incorporate a detailed model for adjudicating combat outcomes. Instead, we planned to stop the game if the teams took actions leading to war; however, we did not inform the players that this would result in an end to the game so as not to bias their behavior.

Even while allowing players to choose from a broad array of tactics, a structured game helped the players to develop and implement their strategy.[8] Having a starting menu of moves with defined effects better enabled the tracking of sequences of actions, their outcomes, and cumulative effects over time. This ultimately improved game play and adjudication, and provided interesting insights about the combination of gray zone tactics that could be employed by Russia and the mix of countermeasures that the West could employ to counter the Kremlin's meddling.

---

[7] We defined gray zone tactics as *ambiguous* political, economic, informational, or military actions that primarily target domestic or international public opinion and are employed to advance a nation's interests while still aiming to avoid retaliation, escalation, or third-party intervention (Pettyjohn and Wasser, 2019).

[8] Although we provided specific actions, players retained flexibility to suggest new actions, as discussed in greater detail later in this report.

Elements of the Game

In the game, the Red team was tasked with remaining in power, expanding its international influence, and undermining NATO unity without provoking an overt conflict. Green and Blue teams sought to defend their allies from Red gray zone aggression while similarly avoiding war. The teams, therefore, were competing over several dimensions which were represented on the game board as the orientation of Balkan nations, NATO unity, and Red regime stability. The gray zone game is a card-driven game with two boards. The first board is the timeline, which is where the teams make moves by placing their cards down in an effort to affect the various scores that are represented on the second board, a map of the region.

Setup: Map, Timeline, and Card Decks
Map
The map focuses on the region in question, the Balkans, and reflects the "scores" or the state of the world for the game. The map has three main components: (1) countries, which are scored according to several values, but most importantly by their orientation; (2) a NATO unity tracker; and (3) a Russian regime stability tracker. See Figure 3.1 for more details.

Country Scores
Each Balkan country that the Red team might target with its gray zone tactics is scored along several dimensions. Two scores in particular are central—the orientation of a country and its governance score. The former is critical because it encapsulates the degree to which the public and elites support either Russian or Western policies. The orientation score is usually the focus of the players, as the Red team seeks to halt NATO expansion and to erode Western influence in the Balkans, while the Blue and Green teams seek to thwart any encroaching Russian influence in the region and draw states closer into their orbit. The latter score—governance—reflects the ability of a state's public institutions to provide basic services, including law and order through legal bureaucratic means. Governance is one of the key factors that determines whether there are openings that Red's gray zone tactics

Figure 3.1
Balkans Gray Zone Game Map

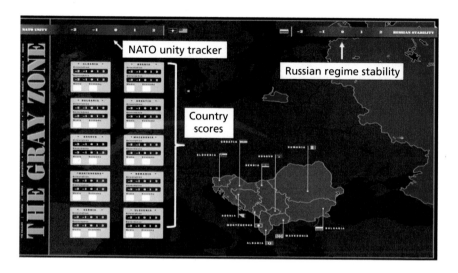

can exploit or whether the state is able to quickly detect and respond to the Kremlin's meddling and prevent instability or internal violence from taking hold. If Moscow is aiming to destabilize a country, either because it cannot shift its orientation or it believes that this is the best way to weaken NATO, then the main struggle can shift to governance. Two other scores—freedom of the media and economic dependence— are subordinate scores that represent key areas of strength and vulnerability that affect the likelihood that certain Russian gray zone tactics and Western countermeasures could succeed.

Each country on the map is assigned a starting orientation, governance, media, and economic score that reflects the initial conditions that teams must consider as they developed their strategies. These scores represent key levers within each country that the teams can seek to influence and embody the inherent strengths and vulnerabilities of each country. To keep the game playable, all scores are on a simple, ordinal scale ranking from −2 to +2. Each country is scored relative to each other rather than an objective global standard. Because the scores are affected by player actions, they are flexible and change throughout the game and are therefore marked in a temporary fashion on the map. See Figure 3.2 for a depiction of how scores are kept on the game board. Because they are focal points of player actions, orientation and governance are given a prominent position, and the media and economy scores are written in a subordinate, blank space.

To score each nation, we reviewed several indexes that rate different aspects of these factors, conducted extensive research on each nation, and consulted with regional experts. When possible, we initially relied on a standard index to score nations along the dimensions of interest, but then we verified, and if necessary, modified these scores using additional research on each nation and a qualitative expert review. This research was incorporated into country fact sheets that were provided as resources to the players in the game. The country fact sheets were short narrative summaries reviewing the current state of politics and governance, orientation, polarization and instability, media, and

Figure 3.2
Country Score Example

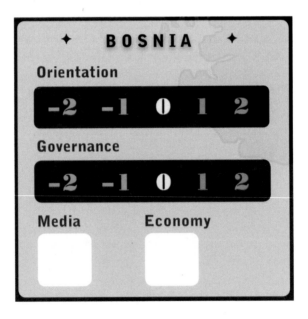

economics in each nation. Finally, we had regional experts review and validate the country scores and fact sheets.

Table 3.1 lists the definition of each of the country scores and describes the key factors that affect the scores and the indexes that are used to assign the values. These metrics were identified as the objects that the teams were trying to affect (i.e., governance, orientation) or as critical intervening variables that affected the efficacy of different gray zone tactics (i.e., economic dependence, media freedom). A single index that measured all of the factors we sought to score did not exist, requiring us to use various indexes to determine our scores. We ultimately chose the indexes detailed in Table 3.1, using the analytical rigor of the index and closeness to the phenomena we sought to score. When possible, we examined multiple indexes that measured a factor as a check on relying on any one index and to increase our confidence in our initial country scores.[9]

Orientation was based on several subordinate factors, including whether a state had deep societal or cultural ties to Russia or the West; overall public opinion toward Russia, NATO, the EU, and the United States; and whether it was a democracy. We relied on a variety of sources because a single index measuring all these factors was not available. We used Freedom House's Freedom in the World index rankings and the World Bank's Voice and Accountability scores to identify whether a state was a strong, consolidated liberal democracy; an authoritarian nation; or something in between. When available, we examined recent public opinion polls asking about views toward Russia, NATO, the EU, and the United States. We also examined key demographic variables to assess whether part of the population had ethnic or cultural ties to Russia. These quantitative measures were then crosschecked with additional qualitative research about individual countries and rolled into one score.

The governance score was tied more directly to two indexes—the World Bank Worldwide Governance Indicators and the Failed States

---

[9]   We identified several indexes that represented the phenomena we wished to score through research and ultimately chose the indexes detailed in Table 3.1 based on the analytical rigor of the index and closeness to the phenomena we sought to score.

Table 3.1
Country Scores

Factors	Sources
Orientation Score: degree to which public and elites support Western or Russian policies	
Public opinion	• Polls of views of Russia, NATO, the EU, and the United States
Ethnic and cultural ties to Russia	• CIA World Factbook
Ties to the West	• NATO member or in member action process (MAP) • EU member or entered into negotiations • Supported sanctions against Russia
Democracy	• World Bank Worldwide Governance Indicators for Voice and Accountability • Freedom House Freedom in the World Index
Governance Score: ability of public institutions to provide basic services, including law and order, through legal bureaucratic means	
Rule of law, corruption, fractionalized elites, group grievances, regulatory quality, political stability, and absence of violence	• World Bank Worldwide Governance Indicators • Fund for Peace State Fragility Index • Transparency International Corruption Perceptions Index
Economic Dependence Score: degree to which the country's economy depends on Russia	
Trade and economic strength	• Harvard's Atlas of Economic Complexity • UN Comtrade Database • World Trade Organization trade profiles • World Bank World Integrated Trade Solution
Foreign direct investment	• Economist Intelligence Unit
Media Freedom Score: degree to which the media reports on politics without state interference, and journalists are safe and free from legal or economic pressures	
Media	• Freedom House Freedom of Press and Media indicators

Index—that rated whether a state's public institutions could provide basic services, including law and order, through legal bureaucratic means. Economic dependence was scored depending on the amount of imports and exports to Russia, the overall strength of the economy, and foreign direct investments made by Russian companies into a country. We examined a variety of resources, including Harvard's Center for International Development Atlas of Economic Complexity, the World Bank's World Integrated Trade Solution, the United Nations (UN) Comtrade Database, and World Trade Organization's trade profiles, to understand trade flows and the general standing of the economy. Foreign direct investment is often murky, so we also did qualitative research looking at the Economist Intelligence Unit country reports, periodicals, and other secondary sources. Media freedom—the degree to which the media reports on politics without state interference, and to which journalists are safe and free from legal or economic pressures—used Freedom House's Freedom of the Press and Media scores.

Finally, several SMEs focusing on the Balkans, Europe, and Russia were consulted to get a qualitative perspective on the relative strengths and weaknesses of each state and to review our relative ordinal scores.

Trackers

In addition to influencing the politics and current states of different Balkan nations, there are two additional scores that help to determine who is winning in a gray zone competition that pits Russia against the West—the level of NATO unity and Russian regime stability. Breaking, or at least eroding, NATO unity is an explicit Russian objective which drives, in part, its strategy and choice of tactics, and provides a sizable challenge to the Blue and Green teams. The maintenance of Russian regime stability is a concern for the Red team, and although creating instability in Russia is not an objective of the Blue and Green teams, it can be a positive byproduct of their choice of actions in the game. Therefore the map includes two trackers: one showing NATO unity and the other indicating Russian regime stability.[10]

Scores on these trackers move up and down depending on the outcomes of game play. NATO unity is primarily affected by whether Blue and Green decide to act together to alter the orientation of a target state. For example, if there is coordination or successful cooperation between the Blue and Green teams, or if the orientation of a Balkan nation shifted toward the West, the NATO unity score would increase. Blue and Green working at cross-purposes, or a Balkan nation becoming more closely aligned with Russia, would decrease the score on the tracker. The Red player could take specific actions—primarily those that influence a state's orientation—to "break" the NATO alliance. For example, Russian disinformation aimed at sowing discord among NATO members could reduce NATO cohesion over time.

Russian stability represents the level of opposition to President Vladimir Putin's rule in Russia. This is negatively affected by economic sanctions, detected Red covert acts, and failed assassinations and coups. For example, joint U.S. and EU sanctions would exacerbate the troubles of the already struggling Russian economy, resulting in blowback from the population to the regime and thus reducing Russian stability. Although regular failures of Russian gray zone tactics could weaken regime popularity, sustained successes as a result of the Red team's gray zone strategy would enhance regime stability. The Red team's ability to flip the orientation of a state from the West to Russia would also increase regime stability. Although the scores on these trackers do not affect the efficacy of player actions in the target countries, they represent broader goals and domestic concerns that the

---

[10] We recognize that these two trackers are incommensurate because sowing instability in Russia is not a Blue and Green team objective. However, to balance the game, we required a mechanic to place pressure on the Red team. Through our iterative game design process, we found that tracking Russian regime stability—where Red, Blue, and Green actions could affect the "score"—was the best way to create this pressure without detracting from game play and our study question.

players have to contend with because actions taken by the United States and Russia in Europe do not take place in a vacuum.[11]

Timeline

The Balkans map is mainly a scoreboard and a planning tool, and game play mostly takes place on the timelines where the teams played the cards that represented their actions. During the game design process, we found it difficult to effectively capture the effects of time: Gray zone tactics can be protracted efforts that are intended to gradually bear fruit, although there are also more immediate and targeted actions that aim to have a more decisive effect in the near term. A traditional game board displays only the current move, rendering it unable to portray both types of actions and making it difficult for players to develop and execute complex strategies with differing time horizons. Therefore, we decided to integrate a two-pronged timeline into the game, where the players made short-term actions in 3-month turns and took longer-term actions in year-long turns. This enabled us to effectively represent short- and long-term actions in the game and track their effects appropriately over time. Additionally, the timelines made it easier to systematically track the effects of gray zone tactics, including how certain combinations of tactics interact with each other.

We created a blank timeline that could accommodate three target countries and consisted of six rows, with two rows per target country or institution (see Figure 3.3). The timeline is separate from but adjacent to the map and is the main place of game play because this is where players make their moves via cards they lay out on the timeline. Cards can be played on either the short- or long-term track of any of the three targeted countries, but there are not distinct long- or short-term cards. However, there are cards that will tend to produce better results on one track versus the other. For example, actions whose efficacy depends on consistency—whether building partner capacity or developing a propaganda campaign—are most effectively played along the long-term track. Additionally, key events with special rules (discussed later in

---

[11] Broader goals include the Russia team being tasked with undermining NATO, while the U.S. and NATO players are tasked with protecting the alliance from Russian gray zone aggression.

Figure 3.3
Gray Zone Game Timeline

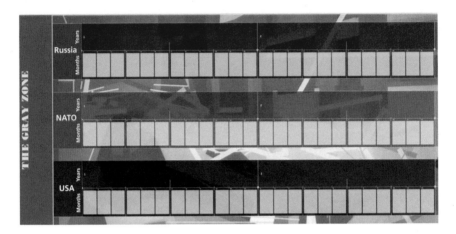

greater length), such as elections, are marked on the timelines in the appropriate spot by the adjudicators as a reference point for players.

Card Decks

The game includes three decks of action cards, each deck unique to one of the three teams, representing the actions the teams can take during the course of the game.[12] To build these card decks, we researched real-life examples of Russian gray zone tactics and U.S., NATO, and EU countermeasures. The decks also included moves made by players in earlier free-form games, which we documented, and included other actions (i.e., actions not defined as gray zone tactics) that the three teams might want employ in a competition short of war. Once these were compiled, we broke them down into three main buckets of activities: social-political, economic, and military-security actions, which roughly follow the DIME categories. See Figures 3.4 and 3.5 for a complete list of action cards by team. As these figures show, the differences between the Red and the Blue and Green card decks are fairly stark.

---

[12] The Blue and Green decks of cards are similar to allow the two teams to work together, but they also include a few unique cards in each deck. For example, only the Green team has the option to deploy internal security forces or to build a gas pipeline to the Balkans.

Figure 3.4
Red Gray Zone Action Menu

DIME

Diplomatic	Information	Military	Economic
• Passportization • Financial support to pro-Russia groups • Assassinate politician • Financial support to nationalist groups	• Discredit politicians or journalists • Fund and promote pro-Russian media campaign • Fund and promote pro-Russian social media campaign • Buy local media outlets • Collect Kompromat on politicians or journalists • Ethnic tension-stoking social media campaign • Assassinate journalist • Disinformation campaign on political figures • Encourage unrest with polite people • Encourage violence or demonstration by proxies • Extol the virtues of traditional values	• Train and equip nonstate actors • Attempt coup • Deploy military forces • Conduct military exercise • Arm state actors • Arm nonstate actors • Harassing air and naval ops	• Disrupt transport links • Expel workers • Attract workers • Targeted sanctions • Embargo exports to Russia • Cut off energy supplies • Raise energy prices • Offer to expand trade • Cyberattacks to disrupt infrastructure services • Reconnaissance of government, media, or economic cyber infrastructure • Purchase key economic assets • Build gas pipeline

Figure 3.5
Blue and Green Gray Zone Action Menus

DIME

Diplomatic	Information	Military	Economic
• Push to expel Russian diplomats	• Fund and promote pro-West/anti-Russian media campaign	• Build partner capacity: intelligence	• Impose sector sanctions against Russia
• Start or restart MAP	• Build partner capacity: local media	• Build partner capacity: internal security forces	• Impose targeted sanctions against Russia
• Build partner capacity: governance, rule of law	• Cultural or educational exchanges	• Unconventional warfare: build nongovernment militia	• Provide economic aid
• Financial support to pro-Western political parties	• Fund and promote pro-Western/anti-Russian social media campaign	• Investigate possible covert action	• Push to diversify trade partners
• Evacuation of green citizens or troops	• Financial support to pro-Western NGOs	• Deploy military forces	• Push to pursue alternate or additional energy sources
	• Encourage demonstrations	• Conduct military exercise	• Offer to expand trade
		• Sell weapons to government	• Ease visa restrictions on workers
		• Deploy SOF	• Cyberattacks to disrupt infrastructure services
		• Provide intelligence	• Reconnaissance of government, media, or economic cyber infrastructure
		• Bolster air defenses	• Build partner capacity: cyber
		• Deploy internal security forces	• Build a gas pipeline
		• Build partner capacity: SOF	
		• Build partner capacity: conventional military	

NOTE: SOF = special operations forces.

The cards represent the actions available to each team described in general terms, to give the players flexibility in how they wished to employ these tactics. See Figure 3.6 for examples of Red action cards. Although the cards indicate a goal, such as encouraging unrest or collecting kompromat, they do not make it clear who is creating the distur-

Figure 3.6
Examples of Red Action Cards

Encourage Unrest with Polite People	Collect Kompromat on Politicians or Journalists	Purchase Key Economic Assets
Modified by: G, polarization Impact on: G CRT: C Political/Social	Modified by: N/A Impact on: Future ability to attack or discredit CRT: D Political/Social	Modified by: E Impact on: E CRT: C Economic

NOTE: N/A = not applicable.

bance, who is the target of this action, and for what purpose this action is carried out. The open-ended cards merely act as a general menu of options, leaving the onus on the teams to explain their intent and how this act fits into their overall strategy. For example, a Red team could play the "encourage unrest with polite people" card with the intent of stoking existing ethnic fissures in Bosnia by creating protests in Sarajevo, ostensibly driven by ultranationalist Serbian supporters of the Republic of Srspka. We encouraged teams to develop a narrative not only to ensure that we correctly captured their move and overall intent, but also to help players get in the mindset of who they were representing in the game and to encourage them to remain engaged. Additionally, the players were informed that they could request a new card if an action was not available within the card deck. Ultimately, the cards are intended to help the teams develop their strategies to achieve their objectives and to implement their strategies over a several-year period.

The basic rules that determine the likelihood that an action would succeed or fail are printed on the card and are therefore transparent to players. The cards detail which country scores are affected by the action. In the example card provided in Figure 3.6, encouraging unrest, if successful, will alter a country's governance score. But this card is also modified by the existing governance score; therefore, a low governance score will increase the likelihood of this action being successful because a weak state is less likely to be able to end violence and protests and restore order. Some cards can also produce certain outcomes, such as instability, although others, such as building partner capacity or developing a propaganda campaign, require incremental investments over time to produce outcomes. Furthermore, some cards do not have a direct effect but rather lay the groundwork for other actions to be successful. For instance, collecting kompromat on journalists prior to playing a "discredit a journalist" card would increase the probability of success for the latter action. However, on its own, the first card lacks any direct effect on the game.

Game Play

This section details how the Balkans gray zone game is played, and discusses adjudication and the feedback mechanisms that drive game outcomes and special rules.

Making a Move

As a part of the first move of the game, the Red player selects three countries to target from the ten Balkan countries detailed on the map. Although Russia conducts "everyday" gray zone tactics in several countries at any given time, it has a limited capacity to conduct sustained gray zone campaigns in multiple countries at once. To represent this constraint and to encourage playability, we chose to limit game play to three countries. The adjudicators then provide intelligence reports to the Blue and Green players so that they are aware of the three countries to which game play will be restricted for the rest of the game.

Each team is then tasked with constructing a strategy for realizing its desired goals. For the Red player, this goal is to expand its influence and undermine NATO unity. For the Blue and Green players, this goal is to expand their influence and defend their allies from Russian gray zone tactics without provoking an outright war. The strategies developed by the teams consist of both long- and short-term actions. Long-term actions make up the crux of the team's overarching strategy, and short-term cards allow the teams to react to the actions of their adversaries and partners, and to capitalize on recent developments. Although teams can modify their strategies, their ability to change their long-term actions is limited to specific times, reflecting the limited capacity of each team to shift course because of bureaucratic inertia and, in the case of Blue and Green, coordination with partners. Similarly, only a set number of cards can be played along each track, representing a finite amount of resources available for such activities. However, there are no restrictions on the number of certain types of cards (e.g., social-political, economic, military-security) that can be played on each turn.

The cards facilitate the teams' development of a strategy and act as prompts for each team's move narrative. When the cards are placed on the timeline, each team publicly briefs out their move. This includes, from their perspective, what their actions were and how they were carried out, what they expected these actions to achieve, and public messaging to both adversaries and allies alike. This level of storytelling allows the adjudicators to link actions that were intended to build on each other and encourages player engagement.

Adjudication and Feedback Mechanisms

Because we built a structured game with a high degree of transparency, adjudication is largely carried out in the open.[13] The cards include a shorthand description of the rules, in particular the factors that affect the likelihood that an action would succeed or fail. This allows players to understand what types of actions were lower- or higher-probability events, given the conditions of the target, and to argue for different outcomes and dynamics in the game when they believed the rules were wrong or failed to capture an important factor driving outcomes. In the Balkans game, when the adjudicators agreed that the rules incorrectly

---

[13] The exception to transparent adjudication was covert actions, which were adjudicated with only the acting team present.

captured the dynamic, the rules were flexible enough to be modified in real time and changes were incorporated into the rest of game play.

Our ingoing principle for adjudication was that all outcomes were probabilistic. This is because most gray zone tactics are complicated, with long causal chains and many intervening variables. Given this complexity, we decided that actions should not have assured results and the game needed to capture the potential wide variety of variation in outcomes. We developed probability distributions using a combination of research and SME inputs from prior games, with a baseline probability of success ranging from 5 percent to 40 percent, depending on the context in which the action was taking place. These probability curves were displayed in a series of simple CRTs that allowed us to shift the likelihood of outcomes in a limited number of ways using conditions in the target country and prior actions taken by the acting team. We also captured the potential cumulative impact of some gray zone tactics, such as propaganda, by allowing for partial success to build, eventually resulting in a change in the orientation score.

In general, a targeted nation's orientation is directly affected by actions that seek to sway popular and elite opinion, such as propaganda campaigns and efforts to promote traditional values. The degree to which information operations succeed, however, is also typically mediated by whether a targeted nation has a strong and free press, which is represented by the media score. Orientation might also be indirectly affected by such other factors as economic policies and economic ties or military actions intended to intimidate or reassure a targeted nation. Governance is affected by a wide variety of actions that tend to fall into two categories: efforts to weaken institutions or a public's trust in them, and countervailing attempts to strengthen state capacity. Examples of the former include campaigns to discredit politicians or assassinate them; foment protests, violence, and instability; encourage corruption; and support paramilitaries. Actions attempting to strengthen governance include a wide variety of efforts to enhance government capacity in particular areas, such as building partner capacity in governance and rule of law, intelligence, or internal security forces. Additionally, if a targeted nation is simply unable to directly govern or provide stability, the Blue and Green teams could directly provide capacity by, for instance, sending investigators or police forces, such as the gendarmerie.

For example, when played, the card shown in Figure 3.7 seeks to build partner capacity (BPC) and, if successful, will enhance the governance score of the target country. The likelihood of success is also conditioned by the preexisting level of governance. This is because more effective governments have a higher absorptive capacity, which is consistently associated with BPC success, and therefore is the main driver of the baseline likelihood that the action will work. Additionally, orientation modifies the probability of success because it represents whether the interests between the provider of BPC and the partner nation are aligned, which is another key factor in determining BPC outcomes. The orientation score has a smaller but still potentially significant modification on the outcome. Although the card itself is purposefully vague to encourage creativity among the teams in how to employ these cards, it makes clear the recipient of the act (e.g., con-

Figure 3.7
Example Card

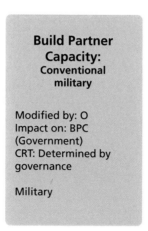

Build Partner
Capacity:
Conventional
military

Modified by: O
Impact on: BPC
(Government)
CRT: Determined by
governance

Military

ventional military).[14] Therefore, although the players are able to retain control over how they will build partner capacity and to what end, the score is not changed by how they choose to undertake the act and other details they might share in their narrative.[15]

After all the cards are adjudicated at the end of each turn, the country scores are updated to reflect the new situation. The final scores are not confirmed until after all actions are adjudicated, so it is possible for several competing actions to succeed, resulting in no net change to the score. These new scores then become the baseline scores for the next round of the game. Small changes to scores in one area at the beginning can have long-term implications for other scores. For example, a change to the media score could result in a change in response to propaganda, which could affect orientation, which could then affect the response to BPC, and ultimately governance.

Special Rules

The game has special rules for certain actions and events that take place in the game. These consist of covert actions, elections, and instability.

Covert Actions

Ambiguity is a defining characteristic of the gray zone. Russia has, on numerous occasions, conducted covert acts in many countries. Similarly, the United States and other democracies also use covert actions to achieve their political aims.[16] To represent covert actions, we needed to limit the information teams had about their opponent's actions and intent. We did so by having the teams initially place all their cards face down on the timeline—in part to ensure that moves were sub-

---

[14] Other building capacity cards in the game focus on unconventional forces, law enforcement, intelligence, cyber, and governance.

[15] In theory, a team could employ a card in a way we did not expect without requiring a new card to be written. In such a case, we would adjust the modifiers and CRTs or the impact as needed. We should note that this did not actually happen during the course of game play.

[16] For more on the U.S. use of political warfare, past and present, see Linda Robinson, Todd C. Helmus, Raphael S. Cohen, Alireza Nader, Andrew Radin, Madeline Magnuson, and Katya Migacheva, *Modern Political Warfare: Current Practices and Possible Responses*, Santa Monica, Calif.: RAND Corporation, RR-1772-A, 2018.

mitted simultaneously—and then flip over overt actions while briefing out their move in narrative fashion, leaving the covert actions face down. This introduces an artificiality of game play because the opposing teams know that covert actions are being played but were not aware of the specific act. However, we believe this is realistic because there is often some evidence that covert activities are taking place, even if the specifics are not known.

When covert actions are played in the game, an additional adjudication is added to determine whether this action will be revealed. The probability of uncovering covert acts is based in part on the strength of target country's institutions, largely represented by the governance score. Furthermore, players have the option of playing cards that can increase their chances of revealing covert actions and attributing such actions to their adversary. These include intelligence sharing or deployment of additional law enforcement. However, uncovering covert activities did not enable teams to automatically stop or counteract these clandestine activities; rather, this required them to play specific cards in response in the next turn. If the covert action was not uncovered, the card would be adjudicated out of the view of the opposing teams and the effects implemented in the next turn.

Elections

Russia has historically employed gray zone tactics to try to affect the outcome of elections in democratic states. The game, therefore, incorporated planned elections in the Balkan nations that were noted on the timeline in the appropriate turn, so Blue and Green players could take actions to protect against electoral interference or Russia could seek to influence the election. In game play, select political and social actions—e.g., disinformation campaigns, strengthening of media literacy, funding of political parties—in the six months prior to elections could affect the outcome of the elections, which in turn affect the orientation of the targeted country. Predicting the outcome of any election is difficult, especially one taking place years in the future. Because of this, we abstracted the electoral process in the game by representing it as a random draw. Additionally, there has been no conclusive evidence, despite its concerted efforts, that Russia's interference has altered electoral outcomes, so we limited how much effect outside actions could have.[17] The possible outcomes are *no change* in orientation, a government *slightly more favorable to Russia*, or a government *slightly more disposed toward the West*. In cases where the electoral outcomes are not in Russia's favor, the Red player could still benefit from second- and third-order effects as their efforts further polarized countries, rendering them dysfunctional and therefore unattractive partners for the West.

Instability

At times, Russia has used gray zone tactics to destabilize a country or to create a frozen conflict to impede that country from joining such Western institutions as NATO. Sowing instability in countries can also create issues for the United States and NATO, further distracting them from other regions, and undermine what many view as NATO's greatest post–Cold War achievements: its interventions in Bosnia and Kosovo. In the game, the Red team might take actions to try to destabilize a target country, which would have a detrimental impact on the country's governance score, but instability is also a special condition that requires the players to undertake additional actions to eliminate. Instability might emerge through deliberate Red actions, such as staging riots, or it can emerge organically in nations that are highly polarized and have weak governance. Countries with very low governance scores are more susceptible to instability, and therefore Red actions that aim to incite violence are more likely to succeed in these environments. The level of instability can vary to include protests, riots, outright violence, or a coup. The Blue and Green teams can take steps to try to avoid instability by bolstering governance. If instability has emerged, the Blue and Green teams must take steps to restore order either indirectly, by building up the beleaguered state's police and security capacity, or directly, by sending in third parties (such as gendarmerie or peacekeepers) to provide security and restore calm.

---

[17] Russia allegedly interfered in the 2016 Brexit referendum, the 2016 U.S. presidential election, and the 2017 French presidential election.

CHAPTER FOUR

Conclusions and Future Applications

Overall, the game design presented in this report met our objective of creating a structured way to think about a gray zone competition in Europe and the wide variety of gray zone tactics available to Russia. Although the gray zone concept remains intellectually murky, we demonstrated that it was feasible to break the concept down into concrete parts and, through structured means, link those parts into a game model. This resulted in a playable, iterative game that forced players to systematically think through gray zone strategies, generated player engagement and discussion, and produced comparable insights across multiple plays.

Although this game produced a great deal of insight, we recognize that it was limited in geographic and temporal scope and in complexity.[1] Although much of this constrained scope was because of intentional choices by the game design team, the aperture of this game could be widened in future iterations. Geographically, the game is limited to the Balkans. Temporally, it is limited to several quarterly turns, and game play rarely covers more than three years, hindering insights that could be drawn about the long-term nature of a gray zone competition. To reduce the complexity of the problem, the effects of combinations of activities are limited within the game. Furthermore, the impact of how gray zone actions build on each other over time is represented in a limited fashion within the game.

---

[1] Key insights and findings from playing this game are in Pettyjohn and Wasser, 2019.

We have, therefore, considered a variety of potential modifications and extensions to the game design to adapt the game for future use. These include the following:

- *Disaggregate Green to better represent intra-European differences:* This game would involve having multiple European teams representing different blocs or subregions within Europe, with different interests and capabilities. Such a game would better let us explore issues of NATO and European unity and gain a better understanding of different nations' capabilities for countering gray zone tactics.
- *Expand the gray zone map to include the Black Sea region:* This game would include active game play throughout the Balkans and the Black Sea region. This would require adapting the Balkans gray zone game to a new subregion of Europe and enabling players to focus on more than three countries at once. This would enable players to have to make tradeoffs to sustain their actions over two subregions with different vulnerabilities.
- *Extend time steps to play a gray zone competition over a longer period of time:* Altering the time steps used in the long- and short-term tracks on the timeline would fundamentally change the game, including the effects of certain gray zone tactics. However, it would enable the players to continue to play the game for a longer period of time and thus gain insight into the nature of a long-term gray zone competition.
- *Adapt the game engine to explore gray zone tactics in other regions*: The basic game mechanics from the structured Balkans gray zone game are ripe to be adapted for other regions, particularly in Asia and the Middle East. We recommend adapting this game to develop a game that looks at Chinese aggression and buildup in the East China Sea and a game that explores Iranian meddling in the Middle East. Because the Balkans game solely focuses on Russian gray zone behavior, we believe that there are interesting and comparative insights that can be gained by looking at Chinese and Iranian gray zone tactics.

This game serves as a proof of concept for a structured, manual approach to serious strategy games. Too much structure forces players to follow only those options laid out by the designers, restricting creativity and ignoring the players' expertise. Too little structure leaves players, adjudicators, and observers adrift with too many options to consider. The scoped, structured approach allows for enough structure to keep discussions on track and provide links between inputs and outputs while still ensuring creativity, flexibility, and transparency. It also allows for the SMEs playing the game to incorporate their knowledge into the game and improve on the initial design. Although the exact rules of this game should not be superimposed over another scenario, the overall design and process can serve as the skeleton for any number of future games addressing similarly difficult policy problems.

References

Bloomfield, Lincoln P., *Political Gaming*, Carlisle, Pa.: U.S. Army War College, November 20, 1959.

Brands, Hal, "Paradoxes of the Gray Zone," Foreign Policy Research Institute, February 5, 2016. As of July 25, 2018:
https://www.fpri.org/article/2016/02/paradoxes-gray-zone

Burgess, Matt, "Here's the First Evidence Russia Used Twitter to Influence Brexit," *Wired,* November 10, 2017. As of August 1, 2018:
https://www.wired.co.uk/article/
brexit-russia-influence-twitter-bots-internet-research-agency

Connable, Ben, Jason H. Campbell, and Dan Madden, *Stretching and Exploiting Thresholds for High-Order War: How Russia, China, and Iran Are Eroding American Influence Using Time-Tested Measures Short of War*, Santa Monica, Calif.: RAND Corporation, RR-1003-A, 2016. As of August 1, 2018:
https://www.rand.org/pubs/research_reports/RR1003.html

Curry, John, and Tim Price, *Matrix Games for Modern Wargaming: Developments in Professional and Educational Wargames, Innovations in Wargaming*, Vol. 2, Barking, UK: Lulu Press, Inc., August 2014.

Davis, Paul K., and Don Blumenthal, *The Base of Sand Problem: A White Paper on the State of Military Combat Modeling*, Santa Monica, Calif.: RAND Corporation, N-3148-OSD/DARPA, 1991. As of August 1, 2018:
https://www.rand.org/pubs/notes/N3148.html

Elkus, Adam, "50 Shades of Gray: Why the Gray Wars Concept Lacks Strategic Sense," *War on the Rocks,* December 15, 2015a. As of July 25, 2018:
https://warontherocks.com/2015/12/50-shades-of-gray-why-the-gray-wars-concept-lacks-strategic-sense/

———, "Abandon All Hope, Ye Who Enter Here: You Cannot Save the Gray Zone Concept," *War on the Rocks,* December 30, 2015b. As of August 1, 2018:
https://warontherocks.com/2015/12/
abandon-all-hope-ye-who-enter-here-you-cannot-save-the-gray-zone-concept/

Erlanger, Steven, "In a New Cold War with Russia, Balkans Become a Testing Ground," *New York Times,* April 10, 2018. As of August 1, 2018: https://www.nytimes.com/2018/04/10/world/europe/ european-union-balkans.html

Goldhamer, Herbert, and Hans Speier, "Some Observations on Political Gaming," *World Politics,* Vol. 12, No. 1, October 1959, pp. 71–83.

Greenberg, Andy, "The NSA Confirms It: Russia Hacked French Election 'Infrastructure,'" *Wired,* May 9, 2017. As of August 1, 2018: https://www.wired.com/2017/05/ nsa-director-confirms-russia-hacked-french-election-infrastructure/

Harlow, Giles D., and George C. Maerz, eds., *Measures Short of War: The George F. Kennan Lectures at the National War College, 1946–1947,* Washington, D.C.: National Defense University Press, 1991.

Jones, William M., *On Free-Form Gaming,* Santa Monica, Calif.: RAND Corporation, N-2322-RC, 1985. As of August 1, 2018: https://www.rand.org/pubs/notes/N2322.html

Levine, Robert A., Thomas Schelling, and William M. Jones, *Crisis Games 27 Years Later: Plus C'est Deja Vu,* Santa Monica, Calif.: RAND Corporation, P-7719, 1991. As of August 1, 2018: https://www.rand.org/pubs/papers/P7719.html

Mazarr, Michael J., "Struggle in the Gray Zone and World Order," *War on the Rocks,* December 22, 2015. As of August 1, 2018: https://warontherocks.com/2015/12/struggle-in-the-gray-zone-and-world-order/

McCain, John, "Russia Threat Is Dead Serious. Montenegro Coup and Murder Plot Proves It," *USA Today,* June 29, 2017. As of August 1, 2018: https://www.usatoday.com/story/opinion/2017/06/29/ russian-hacks-john-mccain-column/436354001/

Pettyjohn, Stacie L., and Becca Wasser, *Competing in the Gray Zone: Russian Tactics and Western Responses,* Santa Monica, Calif.: RAND Corporation, RR-2791-A, 2019. As of November 14, 2019: https://www.rand.org/pubs/research_reports/RR2791.html

Robinson, Linda, Todd C. Helmus, Raphael S. Cohen, Alireza Nader, Andrew Radin, Madeline Magnuson, and Katya Migacheva, *Modern Political Warfare: Current Practices and Possible Responses,* Santa Monica, Calif.: RAND Corporation, RR-1772-A, 2018. As of August 1, 2018: https://www.rand.org/pubs/research_reports/RR1772.html

Schelling, Thomas, "An Uninhibited Sales Pitch for Crisis Games," in Robert A. Levine, Thomas Schelling, and William M. Jones, *Crisis Games 27 Years Later: Plus C'est Deja Vu,* Santa Monica, Calif.: RAND Corporation, P-7719, 1991. As of November 4, 2019: https://www.rand.org/pubs/papers/P7719.html

Trump, Donald J., *National Security Strategy of the United States of America*, Washington, D.C.: The White House, December 2017.

U.S. Department of Defense, *Summary of the 2018 National Defense Strategy of the United States of America: Sharpening the American Military's Competitive Edge*, Washington, D.C., January 2018. As of August 1, 2018: https://www.defense.gov/Portals/1/Documents/pubs/2018-National-Defense-Strategy-Summary.pdf

Wright, Thomas, *All Measures Short of War: The Contest for the Twenty-First Century and the Future of American Power*, New Haven, Conn.: Yale University Press, 2017.